Forward

Fear is the only weapon the devil himself has to keep you from achieving all of your dreams. Fear comes in many forms. The fear of success, fear of change, fear of the unknown. It can take the form of procrastination. It can cause you to stop short. It can be so overwhelming to cause you not to start at all.

When we venture into the unknown it can guide us back into security, comfort and stability. Which is exactly where you CANNOT stay!

I write this as a field manual. It is to be used, practiced and given away to assist others. I am no doctor, scientist, or theorist. I only advocate what I myself have used and learned in my own life. What I will convey has worked for me and if you apply it will work for you. Remember what lives on the other side of fear...Greatness.

What is Fear

As I said I am no scientist. I won't lecture you about all the chemical process going on in the brain. Not as if I even know the answer. I won't tell you that fear is the neurological response to a perceived threat. Even though it is. That means it is OLD! Primal, part of your original programming. Designed to keep you alive, safe and healthy. Created so that you can complete your original program. To multiple. That is, it. Your hopes, dreams and desires, they do not play a role. Except in that they are likely to keep you from your primary purpose, so they must be stopped. This is the job of fear. Very "Matrix" isn't it? To achieve any of that you must confront your fears however they may manifest and on many different levels. Learning a process to do this is essential. If not for confronting our fear we would never have learned to walk, let alone find love or start a bussiness.

With this comes good news and bad news. Which do you want first? The good news? OK.. The good news is that as a new born you come pre-programed with only 2 fears. The fear of falling and the fear of loud noise. Just as a baby horse is programmed to walk from birth, these are built into you. Now for the bad news. EVERYHTING else is learned. Not necessarily bad news, right? What was learned can be unlearn. True... but not easy. Now for more bad news. The longer you have held onto a belief the more cemented it becomes. The more effort it will take to change. Like a big-league pitcher trying to learn to throw side arm instead of overhand, (like he did his whole life). Just because you recognize the need to change, and have the desire, the sheer commitment alone will slow if not stop most people.

But don't give up just yet. Just because you were born with the fear of falling does not mean you will never skydive. People jump out of planes all the time. As well as off bridges, mountains and buildings. You must simply learn a process to being able to take the first step and follow it up. Sometimes it will be as simple as to "just man up". Sometimes it won't. It may take time, but just to begin the process is, by itself an act of courage.

Is Procrastination Fear?

Can you classify procrastination as a type of fear? I believe so. In fact, if the main purpose of fear is to keep you safe and secure, then the easiest way to do that is to keep you inside. Preferably well feed, and lethargic. This is defiantly "safe and secure." We may not think of laziness as fear but if you explore this train of thought for a moment: Imagine you are at home watching your favorite sitcom eating potato chips. You know you should head out and hit the gym. At this very moment you remember that the laundry is piling up, the house is a mess and it is too cold outside to even think about leaving, (short of a house fire). All this may be true however if you drill down Id be willing to bet you are avoiding the pain associated with the sore muscles, sweat and the discomfort that comes with a long run. Your subconscious knows this and is ready to give you every reason and excuse to get out of it. This is fear. The only question is can you admit it?

The most effective way to overcome fear is not to adapt to it but to leave it behind. Once you can really recognize it for what it is, you can begin to leave it in the rear view. This type of fear is not only the easiest to over come but is a very effective building block that you can use on your path to overcome other fears. Sometimes the simplest approach is the best, and purely seeing what is afoot and by recognizing the signs (more on that later) you can simply spur yourself into action.

Nike said it best, "Just do It". For overcoming procrastination, it may be that simple. The harder part is to continue to do it again and again. This is when the discipline takes over. The great news is you only must be disciplined until the habit is formed. Then you're on auto pilot.

When you overcome this seemingly small obstacle your instinct will be to minimize it. DON'T! You have made a step in building you credibly. This will give you more than confidence and faith in your ability, but you will begin to believe that you can and will do what it takes to achieve your goals. This plays a critical role in establishing our process. Do not take it lightly. It is the first of many steps to become unstoppable.

What to Look Out For

The first step in overcoming any fear, no matter if it is a charging lion or calling a bill collector, is to recognize the signs. Knowledge is power. Let me amend that…Applied knowledge is power. The reverse is even more true. This is that the denial of knowledge and action will only serve to appease your fragile ego and you will gain NOTHING. Not power, not insight or achievement. So how do you begin to be insightful enough to recognize this in yourself. Step 1. Become a keen observer.

Most people can easily spot the flaws in other people, but they struggle when they point the lens at themselves. What can you take from this? Foremost that you already have the ability to see the point in which action should be taken and when a decision should be made. Also, that you can see how fear begins to take over a person and how they react to it. Now detach. See yourself as an observer in your own life. What would you say to yourself? What would someone observing from a distance tell you? Start small, it will take practice. Congratulations you have taken the first step to becoming self-aware.

Step 2. Keep tabs on your state. The symptoms of fear are universal but manifest them self at different times. How is you stomach? Butterflies? Is your heart beating out of your chest? Shallow breath? Blurred vision? Test your observation ability by checking your state prior to doing something mildly stressful. Ridding a roller coaster or before a public address. You will become aware of your own symptoms and how-to battel them becomes easier. These types of physical manifestations are the easiest to overcome. (more on that later).

The goal of becoming more self-aware is to be able to interrupt the pattern that no doubt follows. Typically, when theses stressors start your inner demon awakens. (The inner demon is the voice in our head that wants nothing good for you but tries to trick you with what is in your best interest. "Don't do that, you'll fail. Don't talk to him/her they don't want to hear from you. Don't take that job, move there or do this or that.") He sees the chance to grab the reigns of power. If you spot these first, you can stop the demon by moving into a different direction. When you become accustomed to doing this you will start seeing these symptoms as the beginning stages of fear. Your perception is as important as how you react. When you see the butterflies in your stomach as something to look forward to, as a sign of something amazing about to take place then you have tricked your own inner programming. Now take the necessary action.

Step by Step

Now for the meat and potatoes. How is it that I can overcome my fears? Well, there is not one single answer. In fact, there are several answers. Each one will work at different times and on different types of fear, but the first step in all of these is knowledge. Looking at our last chapter you know the signs to look out for. You have also become accustomed to recognizing the symptoms in others and in yourself. The next process is one that works with your ability to using your higher reasoning. You will find this effective in procrastination, and the smaller fears like taking the first step of new project or talking to a stranger.

First realizing that you brain is trying to protect you from the unperceived threat. Knowing this, take a slow look around. Is there an immediate danger you should be aware of? If not is the cost of inaction actually higher then the cost of the action you are about to take. It usually is. Here is an example of how that would break down in real life:

I would like to ask my boss for the day off. Step 1: Recognize the signs. In this case it is the excuses I may come up with, "I should just reschedule", or the procrastination in making the request itself. "I will email the request", or I'll ask on Friday at the end of the day. When I see my self saying these types of things, I know the demon in my head is pulling the strings. From an evolutionary standpoint this makes sense. Standing out risks being thought of as going against the tribe. This is not a good plan for survival. So, fear would kick in to stop you. This is not he case today.

Step 2: Access the viability of the fear. Will I get fired from this simple request? Probably Not! Is it more effective to wait till after lunch, Friday evening etc.? Again, probably not. Should I send an email or am I being a little bitch? Probably the latter. Now what will this cost me. The first is obvious, not getting the day off but there is more. Will I resent my job, my boss and will it make me start to say things like "I have no work life balance, or I work too much"? Step 3: decide on the action: Once you have seen thru the lens of the real world the decision partially makes itself. Get up, walk across the office and make your request. Even if it is declined you will respect you self and gain credibility. This is even more important than the actual request.

You will also gain knowledge that you may not have had before. For example, you may actually need to get another job. Or you may find that your boss is a nice guy. Either way you win.

It can be said to "feel the fear and rationalize it." In example number 2 we take this one step further. This uses a process made famous by Tim Ferris known which is known as fear setting. Let's explain.

Example 2: Say you have a passion for surfing, painting, rock music or any other passion that is not easy to make a living at. You are wanting to leave you soul crushing job and pursue your passion full time. This is a time when fear would stop 99% of people in their tracks and the other .5% would stop short once the pain of failure and difficulties really star to kick in. Step one is still the same. Recognize the signs. Are you procrastinating? You'll try it next year, or when you sell the house and have some extra money. Maybe you think your time has passed. Your too old now, you have bills and responsibilities. Remember this is the rational mind trying to keep you safe. What is the cost of inaction? The real cost. Think in these terms. Have you ever investigated your past and found regret? Perhaps a job you didn't apply for, or a course you should have taken. How many times have you said, "if it could do it over, I would have studied harder, or took that chance"? Maybe a girl you wish you would have asked out on a date if you could have only mustered up the courage. Now do you really want to ad to that list! This is the real cost of inaction. Kind of puts this into perspective doesn't it?! This alone may be enough to take the first step. If not let's go to step 2.

Imagine the worst-case scenario. The Worst-case scenario. First you would be though of as crazy for leaving your job. You may never be hirable in the industry again. Second you would lose the respect of you friends and family who would never speak to you again because you have clearly lost your mind. You would lose your house, blow thru all your savings, have your car repossessed, and end up sleeping under a bridge. You would lose weight, eat out of dumpsters, and somehow develop a crystal meth addiction just to deal with the depression. Which of course makes you more depressed and since you have no money you would have to sell yourself sexually to support your new meth habit. Is that about the worst case you can think of? Feel free to ad something in the space below:

Now what is the likely hood of any of that happening? What about some of it? How could you minimize the down side? Maybe a part time job. Start your passion on weekends. Now the most important part. How quickly, if it all goes to hell, could you "pull the rip cord" and get you life back. In this example Even if you were living under the bridge you could probably get a friend to take you in, apply for a new job and be back to your old life within no time at all. You may be a little bruised up but intact.

Step 3 is the most fun. What do I have to gain? Even if you completely fail you would have lived your dream. You tried, learned and grew. What if you pull it off? A new life all together? Your passion realized? Financial security? The picture becomes clearer the further back you step.

If something like this is your scenario, I would advise you to be prepared mentally for a struggle. I say mentally because you will be tested not in the ways you have prepared for but in the ways, you don't see coming. MLK JR. said "take the first step in faith, you don't have to see the whole stair case." This first step is when you see the type of person you really are. This is where you start to build your confidence and credibility. Welcome to fear setting.

The Physical Side of Fear

How can you deal with some of the physical side effects of fear? These range from butterflies in the stomach, sweating, and dry mouth to an elevated heart rate and virago. You may experience the milder side before a job interview or public address. Is rock climbing on you bucket list? This will help with that too. You may still experience the excuses and procrastination, but we already know how to deal with that.

To under stand the physical symptoms you should understand that in the perceived fight or flight situation that you brain thinks you are in, your body releases cortisol. This slows your metabolism, heightens your awareness and focuses your attention on the single task in front of you. This is done to keep your focus on the threat and keep you alive. Since we know that you are not dealing with a real "loss of life" situation we need to return to base a quickly as possible.

The fastest way to flush out the cortisol is by oxygenating our blood. This can be done by taking several deep breaths in quick succession. All the way into the belly and out. Do these 15 times or until you start to get the spins. It shouldn't take too long. Make sure you don't attempt this while driving. I did it once in the shower and almost fell on my butt. Slowly return to normal breath and allow the oxygen to take effect. With in a few moments you will be focused, and the butterflies gone. This is your window to act. Your brain cannot be afraid and engaged at the same time. Take advantage of the opportunity and get into action. Jump out of the plane, give the speech just get moving. As soon as your done a new feeling will come over you. A feeling of accomplishment This one you will want to last for a while.

Group Therapy

Humans are social animals. Yes, even that guy at the end of the block that has the "No Soliciting" sign. We all long for the connection with others. Its primal. Being part of a group is the best way to ensure our survival and safety. That being said it, it can also be a double edge sword. It is precisely that wanting for connection that can keep us from expressing our true individuality. In ancient times being expelled from the group would be a death sentence. Better to say quiet in the back rather then attempting to stand out. Now you may understand that hermit at the end of the block a little better. However, remember the words of Earl Nightingale, "The opposite of courage is not cowardness, it is conformity."

So, in knowing this about ourselves, sometimes the strategy to overcome a fear is in a group. Take a partner. This is why you rarely hear someone say, "I'm going skydiving tomorrow" It's usually "My best friend and I are going skydiving tomorrow". Precisely why bank robbers are in groups. Its not just the need of a getaway driver. Can you not drive away from the crime scene yourself? No, it's the extra set of eyes to scan for a threat, and the extra set of hands to help deal with that threat. So how can you use this to your advantage?

Example: If you are a door to door salesman (I'm sorry if you are) and you are having trouble getting started, why not enlist help. Grab another sales man and work a neighborhood together. Team up and work opposite sides of the block. This micro step will help you bridge the gap until you can shoulder the responsibility yourself. Make no mistake, this is progress.

The power of the group is real and works very well. It works even better when you combine it with our next principle which is immersion. If you still need proof that sometimes groups help people overcome fear, just count how may people you see solo, in line at a rollercoaster. Go ahead, I'll wait……

Immersion

One of the most effective ways to eliminate fear from a project is thru immersion. Do it until it becomes mundane. A perfect example of this is driving a car. Statistically this is the most dangerous task that people do on a daily basis. However, since you have done it so often it has become boring to you. So much so that you can now TXT, eat and day dream all while doing this most dangerous of task. The odds of you being involved in an accident are 1 in 71 in your life time. More then shark attacks, violent crime and lightening strikes combined. How did you become so brave? Immersion. In this sense all you must do is find the courage to start. (See the pervious chapter) Once you have begun you have to do is keep the momentum going. It takes an average of 66 repetitions to build a new habit. Be consistently brave for 2 months. This comes down to more girt and discipline then bravery. "Discipline is the fuel to keep going until habit takes over." Start with baby steps and continue until fully immersed. The goal is to become so sick of what you have at hand that you want to quite out of pure boredom. This is when you apply grit but that is a different topic all together. Look at the next example:

Example: You afraid of the deep end of the pool because you are a week swimmer.

I am going to skip the first few steps IE recognizing the fear and accessing its credibility as I am sure you have already mastered them. Now I know you think I'm going to say jump into the deep end, but I'm not. That could be the worst thing you could do. (Drowning and all) It may cause you to panic which would just solidify your fear. However, you do need to spend time in the water. A lot of time, EVERY DAY. You will want to spend so much time in the water your hands get clammy and you start to grow gills. You will notice your brain tell you that you should watch a video or read a book first. Although this sound great recognize it for what it is. Procrastination and lies. It is the very thing that has held you back for years. The fact is the longer you spend in the water the more your skill and confidence grows. This will of course increase your confidence. You can read your book and watch your videos after you have gotten wet.

Daily you should inch 1 foot deeper. Use fins if necessary. This is called micro progression. It will also build your confidence and give you credibility with yourself. As your confidence and skill grows remove the fins. "inch by inch everything is a cinch." Immersion can be a very quick way to not only gain skill and overcome fear but could also put you on a path to mastery if this is your goal. In this example your fear was real. Without the skill you have gained you could have drowned. Since you had the courage to face it consistently, and progress father each day you began to callous over the fear and build skill. Soon this will not be something you loath but instead love.

Identity

In our last chapter we will outline a process for leaving your fear behind. Thus far we have discussed short term steps to bridge the gap between the fear of starting, to momentum. Once you have begun to move motion takes over and propels you the rest of the way. That being said, the way to truly beat fear is to not push thru it but to untimely leave it behind. This requires a process. A process in which you shape your identity. It all comes down to how you see you self. You will always stay true to your core identity even if you're not sure what that is. You should not try to create an identity that Is fearless but to create one that can handle situations and adapt to problems and overcome them.

Make no mistake your identity is yours to choose. It may be the only thing that is truly yours and can never be lost, stolen or taken from you. Has anyone ever told you that? I bet not. No one told me either. I was simply born, raised with some core values, made decisions and things happened that I reacted to. From this my personality arose. I had little to no choice in the matter what so ever. Did you know that this simply is not true? You do not have to buy into this model. You can choose your values. You can choose what you like, dislike, what makes you happy, angry or excited. All of it is your choice. Sound simple and in fact it is, however, it is the process of undoing the bad wiring and building the person you want to be. To make this stick that requires discipline and effort.

It is really a process of rebirth. And like being born it can be painful.

The Process

Next, we will outline the process of building a mind that is not void of fear but one that see it as a challenge. A challenge that can be overcome. By building this unbreakable mind you will not just be built to handle challenges but will actively seek them out. This way of thinking is not a quick fix, it requires that you "rewire" your brain. You must get rid of all the years' worth of bad programming. Take on this challenge slowly and completely. Although the change will not come quickly it will be worth it.

Step 1: Credibility

We have covered briefly, but it deserves a second look. Most people lack a certain credibility. Not just with others but with themselves. Your subconscious mind is constantly working and observing. For this reason, your actions establish a level of "what your credibility with yourself is." As an example, have you ever said, "I'll get up early tomorrow early and exercise" Then 6am comes and goes and you decide to start the next day? Your mind takes note of this and you have told yourself that it is ok to not keep your word. Slowly your self image begins to change.

The good news is building your credibility is just as easy. It does however take time. You must make your subconscious mind believe that when you say you will do something that come hell or high water it is getting done. For instance, If I say I'm going for a run then I am going for a run. The world does not exist in which I do not run. There is a world in which I don't get any sleep. There is a world where I break my leg and the doctors says I'm crazy and that I should rest. But there is no world in which I don t run. Doing what you say you will do when no one is watch or keeping score is how you build your credibility. For this reason, it is imperative that you are truthful and realistic with yourself. Which brings us to the second step.

Step 2: Micro Progression

To begin to win the fight with your subconscious don't make small goals and work up to larger ones. Make MICRO goals and keep your promises…You may have noticed I use sports analogies. I use them because they are relatable and easy to understand. In keeping with this analogy, I can explain micro progression in terms of gaining credibility. Let's again set the goal of "I said I would go to the gym." In order to gain and grow my credibility, which will help me to craft my identity and allow me to face my fears, I must go to the gym. As minor of a thing as it may sound the credibility that comes from this is more important to your self-image than you can imagine. This means if I have a temp of 101 degrees, I will be going to the gym. I may have to apologies to everyone later but I'm going. Use the H2O fountain do 10 push ups and go home. But I'm going. This small effort is all it takes to keep the momentum on track.

Since I only set the goal of "going to the gym" not doing a 1 hour work out every day. By simply showing up and doing those 10 pushups, I have maintained my credibility. Now most days almost anyone would do much more. And that Is fine. However, this is not the requirement. As your skill increases you will set the bar higher. Not much higher. Give yourself the opportunity to surpass your goals. This is a great habit to get into. A key to micro steps it not to be tempted to move the bar to quickly or far otherwise you risk falling short. This would be a blow to your credibility, and we cannot risk that. It works the same for writing a book. Start with one page a day. Don't raise it to 2 pages for at least 6 months, and for god sake do not set a goal of 10 pages a day. Even if you can do it. IBM was once the number 1 computer company in the entire sector, and they did it by having the lowest sales quotas and surpassing them. As your skill increase raise your minimum. Since your goal is always reachable you will achieve it fostering the discipline to do it daily, growing your credibility, changing your identity and by default growing your skill. This is the power of micro progression.

Step 3 Plan:

The necessity of planning to achieve a goal whether it be a goal to conquer a fear or to achieve a level of success, is to know what a win actually looks like. This means you must dig deep. Do you really want to make a million dollars, or do you want to live free from financial fears? Do you really want to give a key note address or are you after the admiration of your peers? Since you have begun to be truthful with yourself answer these questions when setting your goal. Then create an outline of a plan. I do mean outline. You do not know yet what path your journey will take you on and I can almost guarantee it will not be the one you envision. In fact, at the end of this journey you will likely not even be the same person. So, remember the plan WILL change but the goal (if well though out) should not. Be flexible with how you get there and have the faith that one step in the right direction is all you need. Just keep making that one step. (Micro Progression).

As you begin to move inch by inch you will move into immersion. As a stand-alone step this can be enough to catapult you thru fear but combined with this process of Credibility, Micro Progression, Planning, and Immersion you will begin to get you use to the uncomfortable situations that use to scare you. You remember that feeling of avoidance to do something in which you are not proficient. You now see that as fear and recognize that this is the opportunity that you have been waiting for. An opportunity to grow and become something that you previously were not. You are about to learn something or do something that you are not accustomed to. As you begin to welcome it as an old friend (one that has guided you since birth) you inch toward it. This is you becoming brave. In this sense fear is the force that alerts you to the growth you are about to achieve. You had this same feeling before you rode a bike for the first time or spoke to a new friend. It marks a place of beginning. Keep inching forward, adjust your plan and repeat. This is momentum. Our next step.

Step 4 Momentum:

The hardest thing to start is momentum. Thru this process we can get moving in the direction that we want to go. The further we move and continue to move the closer we get to conquering our fears. As we can see how hard it is to get going remember that it is very easy to stop. Therefore, it is essential to keep moving. Don't let anything slow down or derail your progress. Since you are now credible you can trust yourself to follow thru on the goals necessary to keep the momentum going. One last thing about momentum... Do not take it for granted. This can be you biggest ally or sew the seeds to your down fall.

Putting it together:

Next, we will illustrate how these actions should come together. We can use any fear but let's start with public speaking since this is the number one fear of Americans. Second is DEATH! What does that say about our society?

During this process of growth and transformation we cannot discount the importance of visualization. Because it is the glue that holds all these steps together. Some may call it belief. However you refer to it, it must be practiced from the moment the plan is decided on. If you goal was to climb a mountain you should see yourself on the top of the mountain. Smell the air, feel the cold. If done correctly you will border on obsession. You will think about your goal all the time. You will talk about it to no end. People will tell you that you have gone mad. If you have not heard that you are insane then you have not visualized enough. This belief is the drive that discipline is made of and keeps you going before habit can take over and after boredom has kicked in.

For public speaking see yourself on the stage. Feel the heat of the lights and see the reaction of the crowed hanging on your words. This is our plan. Assuming we have our credibility, we continue to micro progression.

Start by writing and memorizing your speech. You may say this is still the planning stage and I would disagree. Any time you are in action you are creating momentum even if it is small. Hence micro progression. Next would be practice in the mirror then with a friend. If a friend is too embarrassing as public ridicule may be what you are afraid of, then children. Children give their attention over easily and will hang on every word of an adult. This also gives you time in the saddle. You will learn how to use your voice to harness attention. How to use inflection. You will learn when your mouth gets dry and how to control your crowd. As you begin to master this then adults are next. Small groups a first. "Inch by inch and everything is a cinch" Working up to larger crowds then finally to your goal. This process should not be rushed. Along the way you will see your plan change and failures emerge. If you progress slowly your failures will be small, and you will be able to learn and adjust without losing momentum. If you progress to quickly the failure may be too much to handle at the time and you risk quitting, the only true failure.

As you face each obstacle and gain momentum your confidence also grows. Your fear slowly is replaced by another feeling. One of pride. This is a direct result of the discipline you have put forth. Do not discount it. Which bring us to celebrating our wins.

CELEBRATE YOUR WINS

Before you go patting your self on the back for making it out the door to go to the gym, or standing up and practicing your speech in the mirror, you must truly understand that even if you have set your goals to a level at which they are achievable there will still be days in that you fall short. There will be more on this later. For now, let's look at the progress we have made.

It is important not to take even the smallest of steps for granted, even though this will be you first instinct. "I only made it this far, why should I feel good about that?" This is the inner demon trying to stop your momentum. Just as you move away from the pain of being uncomfortable the joy of a small win should be something you look forward too. The question then becomes how I should celebrate. There are many ways. An extra 20 min of web time. Crossing it off your to do list. Almost anything but, not with that which will set your progress back. An example would be a beer after a long run. I have found one of the best ways to celebrate a win is by journaling your progress. This also gives you a point of reference when looking back. You will be able to see how far you have come.

An importin tip for recognizing when you have cause to celebrate is if you have achieved more then you did the day prior. On the days when I really blow it, I look forward to all the progress I will make tomorrow. This gives me the future to look forward to as well as the feeling that I know I will have, when I CRUSH it.

Failure is not an Option. It is NECESSARY!

Do you remember when you learned to walk? Probably not. I bet you remember learning to ride a bike. Both of times you failed. You failed a lot. You fell, you bumped your head, you may still have a scar. What happened in the end? You learned. You learned from every failed attempted, every bruise and every scrape. Did you over come fear? Maybe, or maybe you just became braver. You became use to the act and moved into unconscious consciousness as you approached a level of mastery. This is how we should view failure. As preempting learning. See it as the feeling you get before you are about to gain a bit of knowledge you didn't have before. View it this way because as you become more accustom to fear, feeling it, managing it and not letting it stop you, fear will always be present. However, if you see it as a welcome sign that you are about to achieve something you have never done before you will welcome it.

As you go from failure to failure in your pursuit to achieve skills and develop mastery you must monitor your inner monologue. You must see yourself as working toward your goal and always improving. If you can make yourself into something antifragile so much more the better.

Antifragile is not tough or resilient like steel which will break under enough stress. Antifragile becomes stronger with attack. Like Doomsday in the Superman comics. Imagine if every time you fall short you became stronger, smarter and better prepared. This is the human condition. Unlike any other machine you become stronger the harder you work. Unlike any other creature you can adapt to any environment you are put in. Your inner voice telling you this can give you the extra effort that you need when you want to quite in the face of failure. Every day tell yourself "I am constantly learning and improving." If this is true about yourself, you cannot be discouraged by failure because this failure ads to your ability's and will allow you to be successful later.

One of the best inner monologues I have ever heard was from David Goggin's aka "The Hardest Man Alive". While going thru Navy Seal Training for the 3rd time (not a typo) on broken legs (also not a typo) instead of telling himself that this was impossible and focusing on the pain he told himself "who in the world would still be going right now? Who could even stand up let alone run? Just you! I must be the hardest person on the planet!" He told himself this and believed it. This is the power of the words you tell yourself. No matter how difficult things got his narrative was one that gave him more energy the worse it got. Become antifragile.

Tips and Tricks

Now that you have a process in place and the discipline, grit and credibility to follow thru on that process there are a few tips and tricks that can give you the edge to stay the path. Some of these you have heard of and they are tried and true methods for keeping your focus. Let's explore some of them.

Daily affirmations would be the first. It is important to start your day with a goal. Affirmations are a great way to do this. It should be the same affirmation every day just as your goal should not change. This keeps you focused on what you are after and you will start moving towards it, pushing thru your fears along the way. This is a tested method that motivation addicts have used for years. And it works! It works by slowly changing your mind set. As you repeat the same thing over and over your subconscious takes note and it becomes you. The person that you want to be starts to come to life.

Journaling is another way to stay focused on your goals. Keep a journal with your goals or the obstacle you are trying to overcome. Update it often with your progress, setbacks and revelations. This serves several proposes. First it is a record of you progress, what works and what does not. It is tangible proof of the ground you have covered.

There will be times when you feel like you have not made and distance towards your goals. This is proof that you have. Lastly besides a record of the progress you have made it can serve as a guide to all those that will come after you as an instruction manual. Update it often.

Vision boards act as a visual reminder of your desires. You should choose the items you put on it carefully. Put it up in place that you can't help but see it. On a mirror, or door. Change your back drop of your cell phone. The same image should be on your screen saver. This is all attempting to reprogram your brain slowly. Instead of having your thoughts and programing emerge based off the experiences you have had, you are now in the charge of what you think, how you act and what you feel. Use these tools to design the person you want to be and the thoughts you want to have.

Everyone knows that compound interest is the most reliable way to get rich. Just as making one good investment followed by another small one can compound quickly. So do good decisions. One small step leads to another and a snow ball effect occurs. This is the same with poor choices. One late night can lead to a missed day of work and a missed mortgage payment and so on. Get this process moving for you. Start slowly and use these tricks to keep you focused and your momentum will snowball with little effort.

Act Like You Can't Fail

Imagine you were transported back to the 10th grade. Your memories and personality remain intact, but by some trick of magic you are transported back in time. What would you do? Whatever you want! You would of course be a strait A student, star athlete, head of the student body and have a ton of friends. Best of all it would easy. Why? Because you already know the formula. You know the rules and you can play the game effectively.

Now take that same mindset to the present day. The only difference is you don't know the rules yet. This is the role of failure. To show you when you are on the right path and when your approach needs to be modified. Since you are attempting something new, your fear will kick in. You can look at models, speculate the outcomes but until you make your first move you can't know if your attempt will be effective or not. If it is BRAVO. If not, your second attempt must be made with as much gusto as the first. You must act as though you cannot fail. Use the new piece of knowledge you have gained in your failed attempt and try again.

This is where fear can stop you even before you get going. Although you must see the fear as a good sign. You are about to get a piece of the puzzle you will need to complete your task. Fear stands guard at the path leading toward your destiny. Every turn, bump in the road and fallen tree is a failure not to be avoided but taken note of.

There is a difference between the courageous and fearless. A solider is courageous. He knows the consequences; he still feels the fear but acts anyway. Fear does not rule him. Fearless is understanding that the consequence of not acting is far worse than to act. In this way not taking action is what is to be feared which is what drive men to run into burning buildings. Courage can be mustered and forced. Being fearless is a deep change in mindset and is an automatic response from one who is in tune with them self. The outcome may be the same, but the difference in the persons mindset is what can make that decision easy.

Evaluation

After each mile stone you have earned the opportunity to reflect on your progress. If you have kept a journal so much the better as it will assist in this process. Look at where you are now and how far you have come. Remember the roadblocks you faced, the failures you overcame and the amount you have grown. Look at the effort and changes to yourself you have made. You are likely not the same person. The fear that once griped you is gone. At least for now. Time for the next step.

This next step involves reevaluation. If you are now at an 8 on a scale of 1-10 congratulations. Now that 8 is your new 1. Start over and move the bar further ahead. For some this will look like shaving some time off your mile pace and others it will mean opening a new branch of your bussiness or moving into new territory. Two things are sure. One, the process you followed before can be repeated, and two, your fear will return (at this point it is a welcome friend) and your new road bumps and failures will not be the same as the last time. Your learning process continues. You will notice that your dedication to your goal will be increased. People will tell you that your obsessed, or insane. This is a sign that you are on the right path. When those who do not share your focus do not understand it. This is a sure sign you are on your way to achievement. You will notice you do not become tired. To the contrary it gives you more energy then it takes. In this way you will not wonder or become warry. Your friends and family will not understand this either. Not to worry. That's why they say "its lonely at the top." Because no one is willing to go thru the transformation it takes to get there.

Hitting the Wall

On your journey there will be some undefined point where you "hit the wall." This is when the effort that you continue to put forth no longer feels like it is bringing results. When you first started the small amount of effort you put out gave immediate results. Now they have dropped off slowly and are almost nonexistent. What now? This is the point in which the winners are separated out. Will you have the dog brained determination and grit to push thru when everyone else would have given up? Can you continue when you see no light at the end of the tunnel?

What will get you over the wall? For some it may be faith in the process. For others it is the fact that they have put to much time in to give up now. What ever it is that drives you forward you must keep moving. You have not reached the limit of your potential. You have only to keep going to reach the other end. It may require you to double your effort to break thru this celling. Not to worry, to maintain is never as hard as to building. Bruce Lee had a quote about reach you limit:

"If you always put limits on everything you do, physical or otherwise they will spread into your work and into your life. There are no limits only plateaus, and you must not stay there. You must go beyond them."

One last tip. You will never fell 100% prepared. You will likely always feel as though you're not ready. Like you haven't trained, haven't practiced, and are not ready. Is this true or is you mind fabricating fears to keep you comfortable? Likely the latter with a small amount of the former. You have the process to put that voice to rest. Let yourself be arrogant enough to believe that you can achieve what you want. Let that fuel you.

Fear of Success?

I have heard this one before. How can anyone be afraid of success? What does that term even mean? It is the same root as the fear of change. When you move in any direction whether it is up down or across, fear has a chance to rear it ugly head. Because you have left the zone of comfort and are approaching the unknown. It is amazing what a human can get use to. Living in horrible conditions, war zones, poverty. It is equally amazing how much that same person will fight to stay there while professing how much they want to leave. They know they are destined for something different but cannot get them self to move. This is fear of success. For with it come a new set of challenges. This is of course the essence of life.

How to overcome this fear? Prospective! Realizing the challenges, you will face are no where near as hard as what is currently in front of you. A future that is full of the same. By coming to grips with the fact that primarily because of what you have been thru there is no one more qualified and equipped to set off on this path. Sometimes it just helps to think of it as a game. "Ok universe, this is what you gave me. Let's see if I can get out of this and beat you." Whichever your approach, apply the for mentioned process.

Honesty as A by Product

It is worth notating that as you take on the process of overcoming fear you will experience growth as an individual. Your perspective will change, and you will become a more honest person. I believe this is because of the confidence and credibility in yourself. As this increases your need to want to "fit in" decreases and you become more aware of the B.S. that you see in the world around you (and that use to be a part of you). When you are secure in yourself the level of honesty towards others (and to yourself) expands. Its not to say that this honesty always follows growth but in most cases it does. However, if one was willing face the consequences of living an honest life that person can use that honesty to jumpstart the process. Since the confidence to face the truth comes thru growth, therefore the growth usually occurs first.

Despite what comes first, the chick or the egg, the result is the same. A cascade effect that can and will leave you looking back and not being able to recognize your life as it was even 1 year ago. All growth is scary. Change can be paralyzing but, to not change is to just await death. Take on the challenge and grow.

Closing

In closing there are a few points to keep in mind. First that fear is a natural reaction to an unknown outcome. If you can reasonably predict that outcome the fear tends to subside. Second, like all the skills you have acquired over your life the more you practice the better you get. This is no truer than in the management of your fear. Third, life takes a certain amount of grit and determination to push thru that breaking point you will face before habit can take ahold. Fourth, the credibility that you build in yourself thru your actions not only shapes you into a person you can be proud of but also helps to give you the belief you need when you engage in self talk.

Lastly, think big! Your goals should scare you. Do not desire to open a business to make $1million dollars. Open a bussiness to make $100million dollars. Break all your goals down to micro steps and climb that mountain one step at a time. Expect to win and if you fail learn quickly and adapt. I always like to end with a quote. Since it tends to surmise a great deal in just a few lines. This one by Henry Ford is not only suited for this purpose but it is something that I wish for everyone to realize for them self. "One of the greatest discoveries a man makes, one of his great surprises, is to find he can do what he was afraid he couldn't do."

www.ingramcontent.com/pod-product-compliance
Lightning Source LLC
Chambersburg PA
CBHW031333250726
48656CB00005B/2113